Mel Mel's Story Rhymes While Identifying Sight Words

Written By Melanie Chapman
Illustrated By Laila Bey

Copyright © 2019 by Melanie Chapman.

All rights reserved.

No part of this book may be reproduced or transmitted in any form or by any means, electronic or mechanical, including photocopying, recording, or by any information storage and retrieval system, without permission in writing from the copyright author, except for the use of brief quotations in a book review.

ISBN: 978-1-970135-28-2 paperback

Published in the United States by Pen2Pad Ink Publishing.

Melanie Chapman retains the rights to all images.

This book is dedicated to my friends all over the world and my little sister. While having my parents help me with creating this book, I told them I wanted the book to be nothing short of fun filled learning from beginning to end, while learning sight words along the way. So, let's flow together while reading some sight word rhymes.

I am me...
and you are you!

I love sight words
What about you?

SIGHT WORDS CHART

I	AT	THE	RAT	LOOK	BABY	MY
BE	HE	FELL	ME	WENT	DAD	THIS
AN	WE	FROM	A	HAVE	BLUE	MAKE
TO	TOO	TWO	SAY	PLAY	LIKE	HI
OR	SHE	HIM	CALL	IS	ONE	DO
WHO	YOU	HAD	HOW	TIME	WHEN	THAT
MOM	HAS	ITS	IT	HERE	IF	AM
SIT	BUT	WILL	FOR	WAS	NOT	UP
GET	BOOK	FOR	NOW	BIG	LITTLE	FALL
ALL	OF	GO	DAY	ARE	LAY	OUT
DID	AS	WE	FILL	HER	BY	WITH
SEE	NO	HELP	HIS	YOUR	THEM	ON
MAY	WAY	IN	SHOE	CAN	SAID	SO
AND	WAIT	DOG	CAT	DOWN	OFF	NEED

We use them every day.
In everything we say.

I have a baby sister who I love to
teach what I learn in school.
Like reading books I think are cool.

Or matching words because
It's fun to do.

Draw a line from the word to the picture that matches that word.

1. House

2. Dog

3. Box

4. Key

5. Shoe

6. Car

Going to school is one of my favorite things to do. What about you? What are some things you like to do?

I really like my teacher a lot.
Her name is Ms. Brooks.

Ms. Brooks
Readers = Leaders

She encourages us to read lots of books.

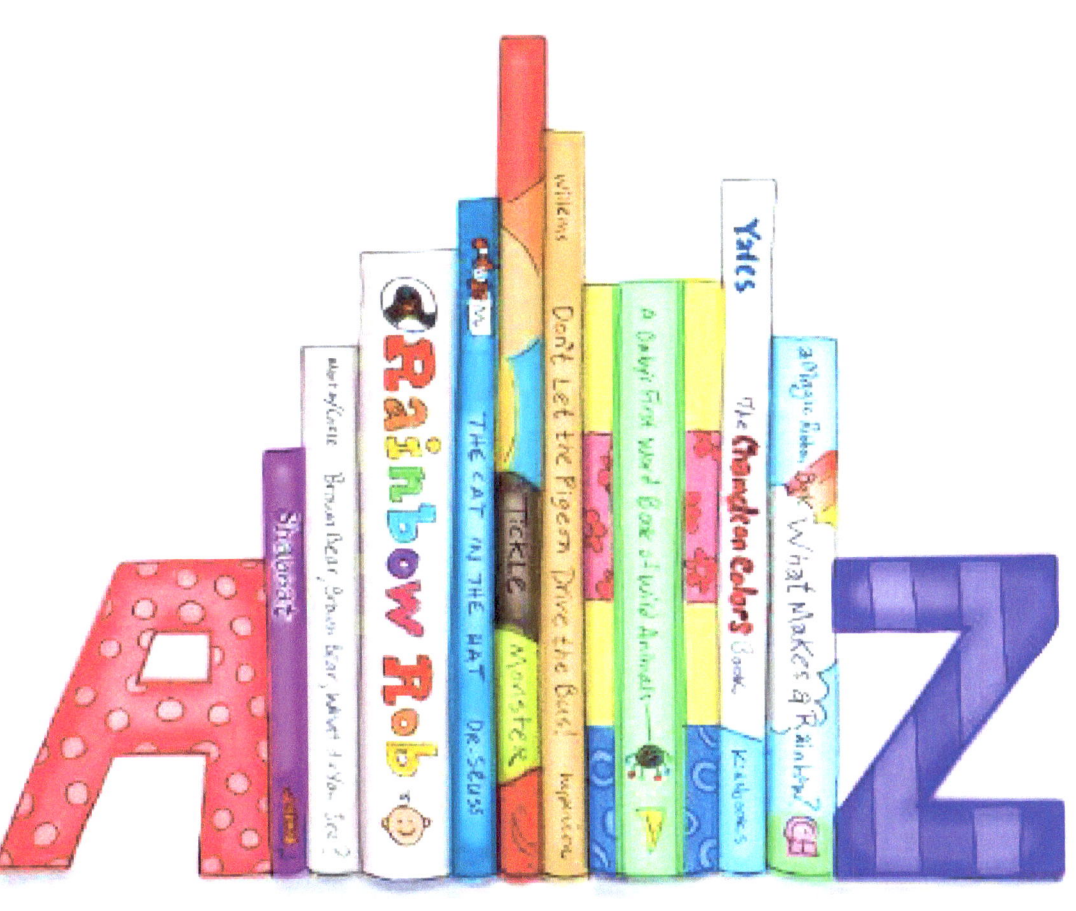

What are some of your favorite things to do in school?

Because it's not all about being cool. We have to remember to follow the rules.

CLASSROOM RULES

1. Listen when others talk.
2. Work hard, and always do your best.
3. Share with others.
4. Use kind words.
5. Keep your hands and feet to yourself.
6. Say please and thank you.
7. Follow directions.

Our parents won't like it if
we just play in class.
So let's learn our sight words,
count our numbers,
or learn some math.

Numbers

1	11
2	12
3	13
4	14
5	15
6	16
7	17
8	18
9	19
10	20

Sight Words

Two	Come
Help	My
It	Not
Baby	In
We	Play
Look	Say
Is	Were
A	Are
More	Who

Math

- $2 + 3 = 5$
- $7 - 5 = 2$
- $9 + 1 = 10$
- $9 - 5 = 4$
- $6 + 5 = 11$
- $8 - 7 = 1$
- $8 + 4 = 12$
- $3 - 0 = 3$
- $11 + 2 = 13$

Whether it's reading a book or riding a bike, we have to pay attention.

In order for us to learn
we first have to listen.

Not to just some parts,
but from start to finish.

Begin at start and fill in the blanks until you reach the finish line.

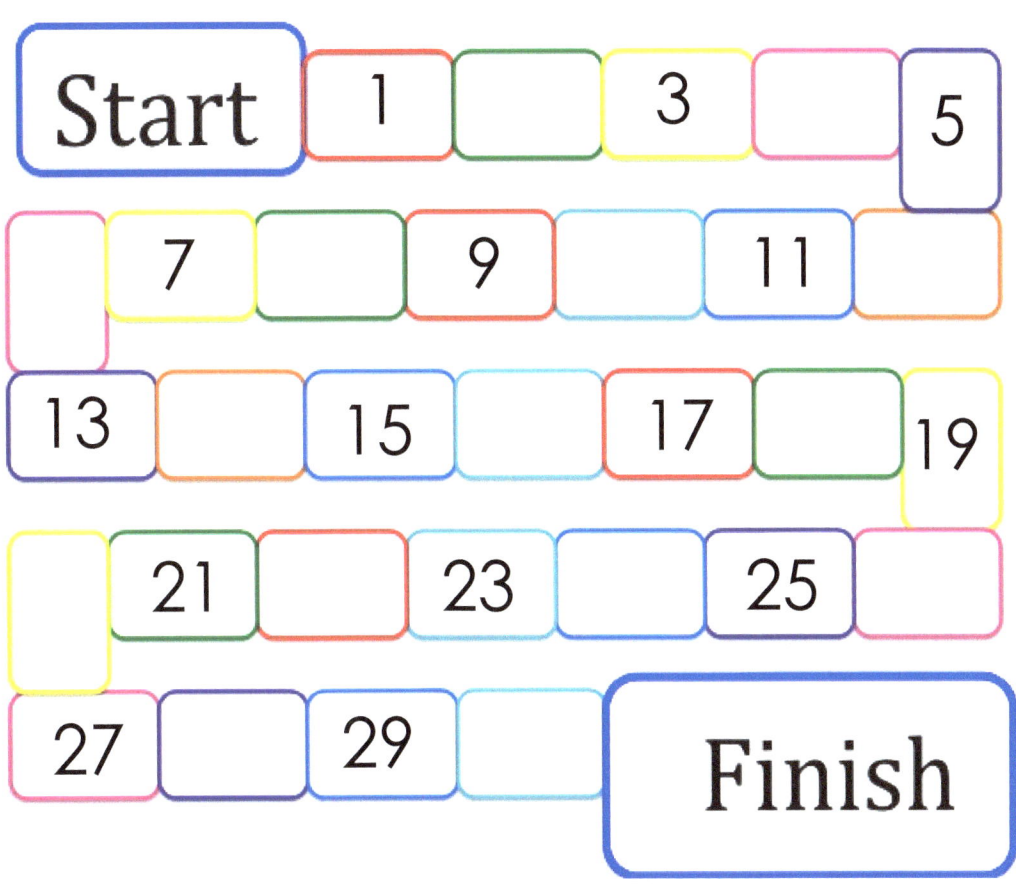

Remember to always do your best.
Even in school on all your tests.

Pop Quiz: Complete the sentence using the correct word.

| Blue | Dog | Bird | Boy |
| Wind | Car | Girl | Are |

1. The sky is _____.

2. Sarah is a _____.

3. Spot is our pet _____.

4. The _____ was in the sky.

5. My hair blew in the _____.

6. The _____ went down the street.

7. Where _____ you going.

8. Johnny is a _____.

So, what are some of your favorite things you like to do while being your best you?

Be the best you, with all you do
and watch how you make all
your dreams come true.

And if you ever wonder
why our parents say its bedtime
know it's because we have to rest
our brains from all the learning we do.

And when they tell you to
put your tablet down
or turn the t.v. off for a few.

Don't feel sad or a little blue.
Instead grab your pencils and
mark off your sight words
or learn something new.

The End!

Pop Quiz Answer Key:

1. Blue
2. Girl
3. Dog
4. Bird

5. Wind
6. Car
7. Are
8. Boy

www.ingramcontent.com/pod-product-compliance
Lightning Source LLC
Chambersburg PA
CBHW041109070526
44583CB00002B/119